Custard and Company

W9-AMN-790

In Memory of

KAREN ANN WATKINS

Granddaughter of
Jane & Leonard
Frank

Custard and Company

Poems by Ogden Nash

SELECTED AND ILLUSTRATED BY
QUENTIN BLAKE

LITTLE, BROWN AND COMPANY

BOSTON   NEW YORK   TORONTO   LONDON

THIS SELECTION AND ILLUSTRATIONS COPYRIGHT © 1979 BY QUENTIN BLAKE

SOURCES FOR INDIVIDUAL POEMS APPEAR ON PAGE 128.

Library of Congress Cataloging in Publication Data

Nash, Ogden, 1902-1971.
    Custard and company.

    SUMMARY: An illustrated collection of humorous poems
on a variety of topics.
    1. Children's poetry, American. [1. Humorous
poetry. 2. American poetry] I. Blake, Quentin.
II. Title.
PS3527.A637C87 1980   811'.5'2   79-25742
ISBN 0-316-59834-8
ISBN 0-316-59855-0

10 9 8 7 6 5 4

BP

Published simultaneously in Canada
by Little, Brown & Company (Canada) Limited
PRINTED IN THE UNITED STATES OF AMERICA

Contents

The Parent

Children aren't happy with nothing to ignore,
And that's what parents were created for.

The Dog

The truth I do not stretch or shove
When I state the dog is full of love.
I've also proved, by actual test,
A wet dog is the lovingest.

The Kitten

The trouble with a kitten is
THAT
Eventually it becomes a
CAT.

The Cat

One gets a wife, one gets a house,
Eventually one gets a mouse.
One gets some words regarding mice,
One gets a kitty in a trice.
By two a.m., or thereabout,
The mouse is in, the cat is out.
It dawns upon one, in one's cot,
The mouse is still, the cat is not.
Instead of Pussy, says one's spouse,
One should have bought another mouse.

The Germ

A mighty creature is the germ,
Though smaller than the pachyderm.
His customary dwelling place
Is deep within the human race.
His childish pride he often pleases
By giving people strange diseases.
Do you, my poppet, feel infirm?
You probably contain a germ.

It's Never Fair Weather

I do not like the winter wind
That whistles from the North.
My upper teeth and those beneath,
They jitter back and forth.
Oh, some are hanged, and some are skinned,
And others face the winter wind.

I do not like the summer sun
That scorches the horizon.
Though some delight in Fahrenheit,
To me it's deadly pizen.
I think that life would be more fun
Without the simmering summer sun.

I do not like the signs of spring,
The fever and the chills,
The icy mud, the puny bud,
The frozen daffodils.
Let other poets gaily sing;
I do not like the signs of spring.

I do not like the foggy fall
That strips the maples bare;
The radiator's mating call,
The dank, rheumatic air;
I fear that taken all in all,
I do not like the foggy fall.

The winter sun, of course, is kind,
And summer's wind a savior,
And I'll merrily sing of fall and spring
When they're on their good behavior.
But otherwise I see no reason
To speak in praise of any season.

The Pizza

Look at itsy-bitsy Mitzi!
See her figure slim and ritzy!
She eatsa
Pizza!
Greedy Mitzi!
She no longer itsy-bitsy!

The Parsnip

The parsnip, children, I repeat,
Is simply an anemic beet.
Some people call the parsnip edible;
Myself, I find this claim incredible.

Celery

Celery, raw,
Develops the jaw,
But celery, stewed,
Is more quietly chewed.

Mustard

I'm mad about mustard –
Even on custard.

Between Birthdays

My birthdays take so long to start.
They come along a year apart.
It's worse than waiting for a bus;
I fear I used to fret and fuss,
But now, when by impatience vexed
Between one birthday and the next,
I think of all that I have seen
That keeps on happening in between.
The songs I've heard, the things I've done,
Make my un-birthdays not so un-

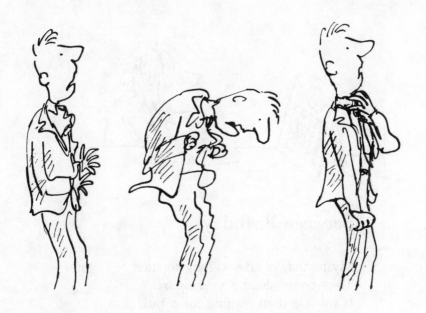

Can I Get You a Glass of Water?

or

Please Close the Glottis After You

One trouble with a cough,
It never quite comes off.
Just when you think you're through coughing
There's another cough in the offing.
Like the steps of a moving stair
There is always another cough there.
When you think you are through with the spasm
And will plunge into sleep like a chasm,
All of a sudden, quickly,
Your throat gets tickly.

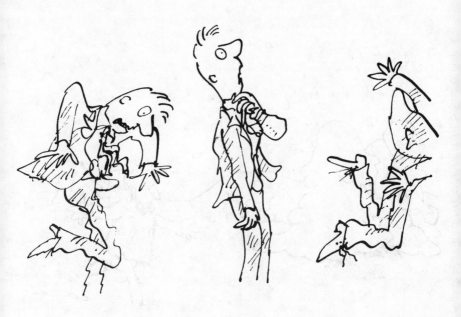

What is this thing called a cough
That never quite comes off?
Well, the dictionary says it's an expulsion of air from
the lungs with violent effort and noise produced by
abrupt opening of the glottis,
To which I can only reply, Glottis-schmottis!
Not that I reject the glottis theory, indeed I pride
myself on the artistry
Of my glottistry
But there is a simpler definition with which I freely
present you:
A cough is something that you yourself can't help,
but everybody else does on purpose just to
torment you.

Winter Morning

Winter is the king of showmen,
Turning tree stumps into snow men
And houses into birthday cakes
And spreading sugar over lakes.
Smooth and clean and frosty white,
The world looks good enough to bite.
That's the season to be young,
Catching snowflakes on your tongue.

Snow is snowy when it's snowing,
I'm sorry it's slushy when it's going.

Jack Do-Good-for-Nothing

A cursory nursery tale
for tot-baiters

Once there was a kindhearted lad named
    Jack Do-Good-for-Nothing, the only son of a
    poor widow whom creditors did importune,
So he set out in the world to make his fortune.
His mother's blessing and a crust of bread was
    his only stake,
And pretty soon he saw a frog that was about to be
    devoured by a snake.

And he rescued the frog and drove the snake away,
And the frog vowed gratitude to its dying day,
And a little later on in his walk,
Why, he saw a little red hen about to be carried off
   by a hawk,
And he rescued the little red hen and drove the
   hawk away,

And the little red hen vowed that whenever he was
   in trouble his kindness she would repay,
And he walked a few more country blocks,
And he saw a bunny rabbit about to be gobbled up
   by a fox,
And he rescued the bunny rabbit before the fox
   could fall on it,
And the bunny rabbit thanked Jack and told him
   any time he needed help, just to call on it,

And after all this rescuing, Jack was huffing
    and puffing,
And a little farther on the snake and the hawk and
    the fox jumped him, and out of him they beat
    the stuffing;
They even stole his crust of bread and each ate a
    third of it,
And the frog and the little red hen and the bunny
    rabbit said they were very sorry when they heard of it.
You see, Jack against a cardinal rule of conduct had
    been a trangressor:
Never befriend the oppressed unless you are prepared
    to take on the oppressor.

The Panda

I love the Baby Giant Panda;
I'd welcome one to my veranda.
I never worry, wondering maybe
Whether it isn't Giant Baby;
I leave such matters to the scientists:
The Giant Baby – and Baby Giantists.
I simply wish a julep and a
Giant Baby Giant Panda.

The Cobra

This creature fills its mouth with venom
And walks upon its duodenum.
He who attempts to tease the cobra
Is soon a sadder he, and sobra.

The Turtle

The turtle lives 'twixt plated decks
Which practically conceal its sex.
I think it clever of the turtle
In such a fix to be so fertile.

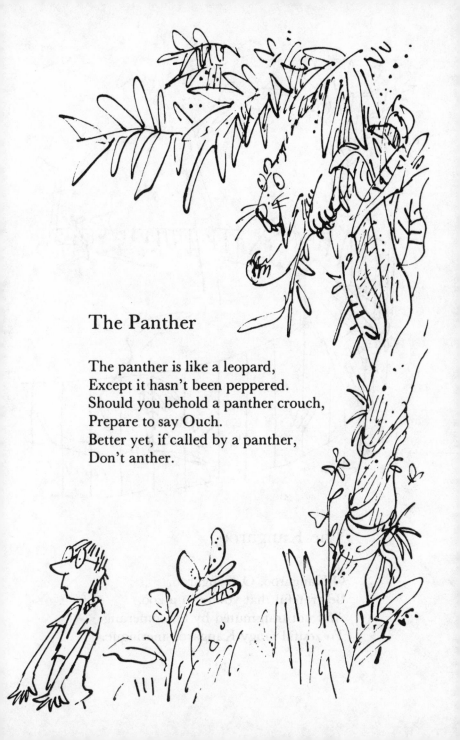

The Panther

The panther is like a leopard,
Except it hasn't been peppered.
Should you behold a panther crouch,
Prepare to say Ouch.
Better yet, if called by a panther,
Don't anther.

The Kangaroo

O Kangaroo, O Kangaroo,
Be grateful that you're in a zoo,
And not transmuted by a boomerang
To zestful tangy Kangaroo meringue.

The Ostrich

The ostrich roams the great Sahara.
Its mouth is wide, its neck is narra.
It has such long and lofty legs,
I'm glad it sits to lay its eggs.

The Canary

The song of canaries
Never varies,
And when they're molting
They're pretty revolting.

The Rhinoceros

The rhino is a homely beast,
For human eyes he's not a feast.
Farewell, farewell, you old rhinoceros,
I'll stare at something less prepoceros.

The Hippopotamus

Behold the hippopotamus!
We laugh at how he looks to us,
And yet in moments dank and grim
I wonder how we look to him.
Peace, peace, thou hippopotamus!
We really look all right to us,
As you no doubt delight the eye
Of other hippopotami.

The Toucan

The toucan's profile if prognathous,
Its person is a thing of bathos.
If even I can tell a toucan
I'm reasonably sure that you can.

The Camel

The camel has a single hump;
The dromedary, two;
Or else the other way around.
I'm never sure. Are you?

The Wendigo

The Wendigo,
The Wendigo!
Its eyes are ice and indigo!
Its blood is rank and yellowish!
Its voice is hoarse and bellowish!
Its tentacles are slithery,
And scummy,
Slimy,
Leathery!
Its lips are hungry blubbery,
And smacky,
Sucky,
Rubbery!

The Wendigo,
The Wendigo!
I saw it just a friend ago!
Last night it lurked in Canada;
Tonight, on your veranada!
As you are lolling hammockwise
It contemplates you stomachwise.
You loll,
It contemplates,
It lollops.
The rest is merely gulps and gollops.

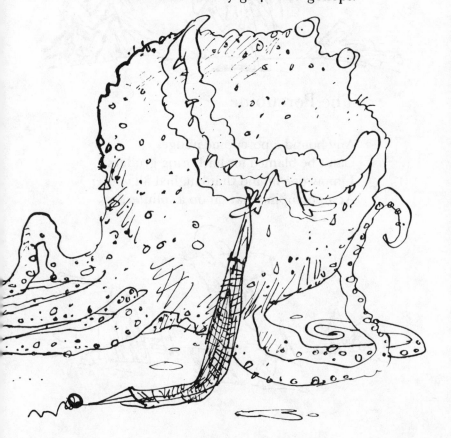

The Porcupine

Any hound a porcupine nudges
Can't be blamed for harboring grudges.
I know one hound that laughed all winter
At a porcupine that sat on a splinter.

Everybody Tells Me Everything

I find it difficult to enthuse
Over the current news.
Just when you think that at least the outlook is so
  black that it can grow no blacker, it worsens,
And that is why I do not like the news, because
  there has never been an era when so many things
  were going so right for so many of the wrong
  persons.

Tableau At Twilight

I sit in the dusk. I am all alone.
Enter a child and an ice-cream cone.

A parent is easily beguiled
By sight of this coniferous child.

The friendly embers warmer gleam,
The cone begins to drip ice-cream.

Cones are composed of many a vitamin.
My lap is not the place to bitamin.

Although my raiment is not chinchilla,
I flinch to see it become vanilla.

Coniferous child, when vanilla melts
I'd rather it melted somewhere else.

Exit child with remains of cone.
I sit in the dusk. I am all alone,

Muttering spells like an angry Druid,
Alone, in the dusk, with the cleaning fluid.

The Tale of Custard the Dragon

Belinda lived in a little white house,
With a little black kitten and a little gray mouse,
And a little yellow dog and a little red wagon,
And a realio, trulio, little pet dragon.

Now the name of the little black kitten was Ink,
And the little gray mouse, she called her Blink,
And the little yellow dog was sharp as Mustard,
But the dragon was a coward, and she called
  him Custard.

Custard the dragon had big sharp teeth,
And spikes on top of him and scales underneath,
Mouth like a fireplace, chimney for a nose,
And realio, trulio daggers on his toes.

Belinda was as brave as a barrel full of bears,
And Ink and Blink chased lions down the stairs,
Mustard was as brave as a tiger in a rage,
But Custard cried for a nice safe cage.

Belinda tickled him, she tickled him unmerciful,
Ink, Blink and Mustard, they rudely called him
    Percival,
They all sat laughing in the little red wagon
At the realio, trulio, cowardly dragon.

Belinda giggled till she shook the house,
And Blink said Weeck! which is giggling for a mouse,
Ink and Mustard rudely asked his age,
When Custard cried for a nice safe cage.

Suddenly, suddenly they heard a nasty sound,
And Mustard growled, and they all looked around.
Meowch! cried Ink, and Ooh! cried Belinda,
For there was a pirate, climbing in the winda.

Pistol in his left hand, pistol in his right,
And he held in his teeth a cutlass bright,
His beard was black, one leg was wood;
It was clear that the pirate meant no good.

Belinda paled, and she cried Help! Help!
But Mustard fled with a terrified yelp,
Ink trickled down to the bottom of the household,
And little mouse Blink strategically mouseholed.

But up jumped Custard, snorting like an engine,
Clashed his tail like irons in a dungeon,
With a clatter and a clank and a jangling squirm,
He went at the pirate like a robin at a worm.

The pirate gaped at Belinda's dragon,
And gulped some grog from his pocket flagon,
He fired two bullets, but they didn't hit,
And Custard gobbled him, every bit.

Belinda embraced him, Mustard licked him,
No one mourned for his pirate victim.
Ink and Blink in glee did gyrate
Around the dragon that ate the pirate.

But presently up spoke little dog Mustard,
I'd have been twice as brave if I hadn't been
    flustered.
And up spoke Ink and up spoke Blink,
We'd have been three times as brave, we think,
And Custard said, I quite agree
That everybody is braver than me.

Belinda still lives in her little white house,
With her little black kitten and her little gray mouse,
And her little yellow dog and her little red wagon,
And her realio, trulio little pet dragon.

Belinda is as brave as a barrel full of bears,
And Ink and Blink chase lions down the stairs,
Mustard is as brave as a tiger in a rage,
But Custard keeps crying for a nice safe cage.

The Termite

Some primal termite knocked on wood
And tasted it, and found it good,
And that is why your Cousin May
Fell through the parlor floor today.

47

Fame was a claim of Uncle Ed's,
Simply because he had three heads,
Which, if he'd only had a third of,
I think he would never have been heard of.

I often grieve for Uncle Hannibal
Who inadvertently became a cannibal.
He asked Aunt Mary to roast him the gobbler;
She understood him to say, the cobbler.

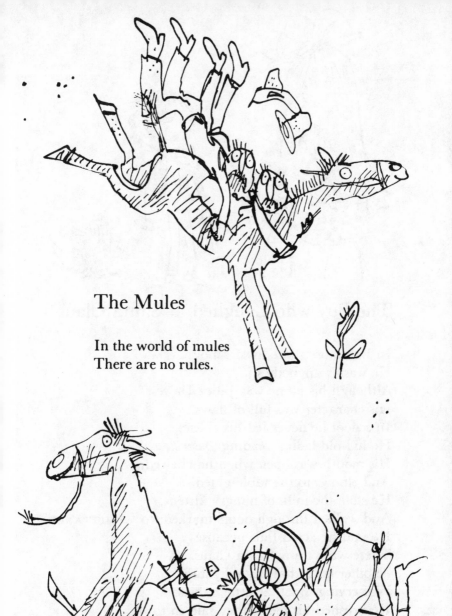

The Mules

In the world of mules
There are no rules.

The Boy who Laughed at Santa Claus

In Baltimore there lived a boy.
He wasn't anybody's joy.
Although his name was Jabez Dawes,
His character was full of flaws.
In school he never led his classes,
He hid old ladies' reading glasses,
His mouth was open when he chewed,
And elbows to the table glued.
He stole the milk of hungry kittens,
And walked through doors marked NO ADMITTANCE.
He said he acted thus because
There wasn't any Santa Claus.
Another trick that tickled Jabez
Was crying 'Boo!' at little babies.
He brushed his teeth, they said in town,
Sideways instead of up and down.

Yet people pardoned every sin,
And viewed his antics with a grin,
Till they were told by Jabez Dawes,
'There isn't any Santa Claus!'
Deploring how he did behave,
His parents swiftly sought their grave.
They hurried through the portals pearly,
And Jabez left the funeral early.

Like whooping cough, from child to child,
He sped to spread the rumor wild:
'Sure as my name is Jabez Dawes
There isn't any Santa Claus!'
Slunk like a weasel or a marten
Through nursery and kindergarten,
Whispering low to every tot,
'There isn't any, no there's not!'

The children wept all Christmas eve
And Jabez chortled up his sleeve.
No infant dared hang up his stocking
For fear of Jabez' ribald mocking.
He sprawled on his untidy bed,
Fresh malice dancing in his head,
When presently with scalp-a-tingling,
Jabez heard a distant jingling;
He heard the crunch of sleigh and hoof
Crisply alighting on the roof.

What good to rise and bar the door?
A shower of soot was on the floor.
What was beheld by Jabez Dawes?
The fireplace full of Santa Claus!
Then Jabez fell upon his knees
With cries of 'Don't,' and 'Pretty please.'
He howled, 'I don't know where you read it,
But anyhow, I never said it!'

'Jabez,' replied the angry saint,
'It isn't I, it's you that ain't.
Although there is a Santa Claus,
There isn't any Jabez Dawes!'

Said Jabez then with impudent vim,
'Oh, yes there is, and I am him!
Your magic don't scare me, it doesn't' –
And suddenly he found he wasn't!

From grimy feet to grimy locks,
Jabez became a Jack-in-the-box,
An ugly toy with springs unsprung,
Forever sticking out his tongue.
The neighbors heard his mournful squeal;
They searched for him, but not with zeal.

No trace was found of Jabez Dawes,
Which led to thunderous applause,
And people drank a loving cup
And went and hung their stockings up.

All you who sneer at Santa Claus,
Beware the fate of Jabez Dawes,
The saucy boy who mocked the saint.
Donner and Blitzen licked off his paint.

The Sniffle

In spite of her sniffle,
Isabel's chiffle.
Some girls with a sniffle
Would be weepy and tiffle;
They would look awful,
Like a rained-on waffle,
But Isabel's chiffle
In spite of her sniffle.
Her nose is more red
With a cold in her head,
But then, to be sure,
Her eyes are bluer.
Some girls with a snuffle,
Their tempers are uffle,
But when Isabel's snivelly
She's snivelly civilly,
And when she is snuffly
She's perfectly luffly.

To a Small Boy Standing on My Shoes While I am Wearing Them

Let's straighten this out, my little man,
And reach an agreement if we can.
I entered your door as an honored guest.
My shoes are shined and my trousers are pressed,
And I won't stretch out and read you the funnies
And I won't pretend that we're Easter bunnies.
If you must get somebody down on the floor,
What do you think your parents are for?
I do not like the things that you say
And I hate the games that you want to play.
No matter how frightfully hard you try,
We've little in common, you and I.
The interest I take in my neighbor's nursery
Would have to grow, to be even cursory,
And I would that performing sons and nephews
Were carted away with the daily refuse,
And I hold that frolicsome daughters and nieces
Are ample excuse for breaking leases.
You may take a sock at your daddy's tummy,
Or climb all over your doting mummy,
But keep your attentions to me in check,
Or, sonny boy, I will wring your neck.
A happier man today I'd be
Had someone wrung it ahead of me.

Epistle to the Olympians

Dear parents, I write you this letter
Because I thought I'd better;
Because I would like to know
Exactly which way to grow.

My milk I will leave undrunk
If you'd rather have me shrunk,
If your love it will further kindle,
I'll do my best to dwindle;

Or, on the other hand,
Do you wish me to expand?
I'll stuff like a greedy rajah
If you really want me larger.

All that I ask of you
Is to tell me which to do;
To whisper in accents mild
The proper size for a child.

I get so very confused
By the chidings commonly used.
Am I really such a dunce
As to err two ways at once?

When one mood you are in,
My bigness is a sin:
'Oh what a silly thing to do
For a great big girl like you!'

But then another time
Smallness is my crime:
'Stop doing whatever you're at;
You're far too little for that!'

Kind parents, be so kind
As to kindly make up your mind
And whisper in accents mild
The proper size for a child.

I'll Get One Tomorrow

Barber, barber, come and get me;
Hairy torrents irk and fret me.
Hair and hair again appears,
And climbs like ivy round my ears;
Hair across my collar gambols;
Down my neck it wayward ambles;
Ever down it trips and trickles,
Yes, and where it trips, it tickles.
Barber dear, I wish I knew
Why I do not visit you,
Why I grudge the minutes ten
In your sanitary den,
Why I choose to choke on hair
Rather than to mount your chair.
Men no busier than I
Weekly to your office hie;

Men no braver than myself
Confront the armory on your shelf;
Men no wealthier than me
Gladly meet your modest fee,
And for a multiple of a dollar
Keep the jungle off their collar.
I alone am shy and flustered,
A solitary, cowardly custard,
Shaggy as a prize Angora,
Overrun with creeping flora.
Barber, barber, you're in luck;
The bell has rung, the hour has struck.
Sloth is strong, but hair is stronger;
I cannot stand it any longer.
Barber, barber, here I come;
Shake up the odorous bay rum;
Bring on your shears, your scythes, your snippers,
Bring on your crisp, electric clippers;

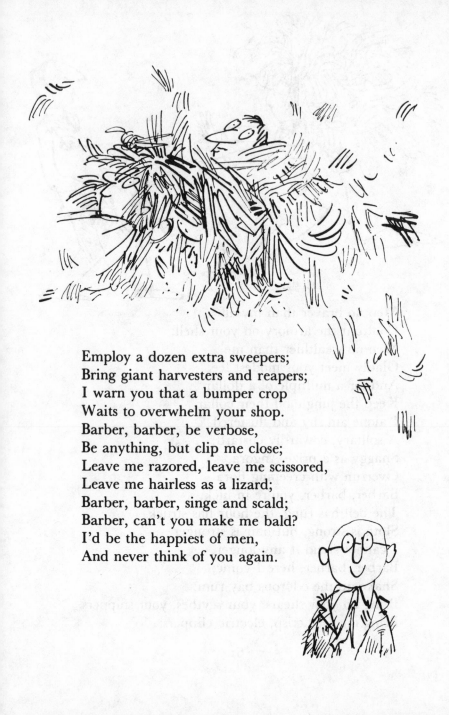

Employ a dozen extra sweepers;
Bring giant harvesters and reapers;
I warn you that a bumper crop
Waits to overwhelm your shop.
Barber, barber, be verbose,
Be anything, but clip me close;
Leave me razored, leave me scissored,
Leave me hairless as a lizard;
Barber, barber, singe and scald;
Barber, can't you make me bald?
I'd be the happiest of men,
And never think of you again.

The Beefburger

In mortal combat I am joined
With monstrous words wherever coined.
'Beefburger' is a term worth hating,
Both fraudulent and infuriating,
Contrived to foster the belief
That only beefburgers are made of beef,
Implying with shoddy flim and flam
That hamburgers are made of ham.

There was an old man in a trunk,
Who inquired of his wife, 'Am I drunk?'
She replied with regret,
'I'm afraid so, my pet.'
And he answered, 'It's just as I thunk.'

There was a young lady named Harris,
Whom nothing could ever embarras,
Till the bath salts one day
In the tub where she lay
Turned out to be plaster of Paris.

The Clean Platter

Some singers sing of women's eyes,
And some of women's lips,
Refined ones praise their gentle ways,
And coarse ones hymn their hips.
The Oxford Book of English Verse
Is lush with lyrics tender;
A poet, I guess, is more or less,
Preoccupied with gender.
Yet I, though custom call me crude,
Prefer to sing in praise of food.

Food.
Yes, food,
Just any old kind of food.
Pooh for the cook,
And pooh for the price!
Some of it's nicer but all of it's nice.
Pheasant is pleasant, of course,
And terrapin, too, is tasty,
Lobster I freely endorse,
In paté or patty or pastry.
But there's nothing the matter with butter,
And nothing the matter with jam,
And the warmest of greetings I utter
To the muffin, the ham, and the yam.
For they're food,
All food,

And I think very highly of food.
Though I'm broody at times
When bothered by rhymes,
I brood
On food.

Some painters paint the sapphire sea,
And some the gathering storm.
Others portray young lambs at play,
But most, the female form.
'Twas trite in that primeval dawn
When painting got its start,
That a lady with her garments on
Is Life, but is she Art?
By undraped nymphs
I am not wooed;
I'd rather painters painted food.

Food,
Just food,
Just any old kind of food.
Let it be sour
Or let it be sweet,
As long as you're sure it is something to eat.
Just purloin a sirloin, my pet,
If you'd win a devotion incredible;
And asparagus tips vinaigrette,
Or anything else that is edible.
Bring salad or sausage or scone,
A berry or even a beet,
Bring an oyster, an egg, or a bone,
As long as it's something to eat.
If it's food,
It's food;
Never mind what kind of food.
Through thick and through thin
I am constantly in
The mood
For food.

You and Me and P. B. Shelley

What is life? Life is stepping down a step
    or sitting in a chair,
And it isn't there.
Life is not having been told that the man has just
    waxed the floor,
It is pulling doors marked Push and pushing doors
    marked Pull and not noticing notices which say
    'Please Use Other Door.'
Life is an Easter Parade
In which you whisper: 'No darling, if it's a boy we'll
    name him after your father!' into the ear of
    an astonished stranger because the lady you thought
    was walking beside you has stopped to gaze into
    a window full of radishes and hot malted
    lemonade.

It is when you diagnose a sore throat as an unprepared
geography lesson and send your child weeping to school
only to be returned an hour later covered with spots
that are indubitably genuine,
It is a concert with a trombone soloist filling in for
Yehudi Menuhin.
Were it not for frustration and humiliation
I suppose the human race would get ideas above
its station.
Somebody once described Shelley as a beautiful
and ineffective angel beating his luminous wings
against the void in vain,
Which is certainly describing with might and main,
But probably means that we are all brothers under
our pelts,
And Shelley went around pulling doors marked Push
and pushing doors marked Pull just like everybody else.

Don't Cry, Darling, It's Blood All Right

Whenever poets want to give you the idea that
    something is particularly meek and mild,
They compare it to a child,
Thereby proving that though poets with poetry may
    be rife
They don't know the facts of life.
If of compassion you desire either a tittle or a jot,
Don't try to get it from a tot.
Hard-boiled, sophisticated adults like me and you
May enjoy ourselves thoroughly with *Little Women* and
    Winnie-the-Pooh,
But innocent infants these titles from their reading
    course eliminate
As soon as they discover that it was honey and nuts
    and mashed potatoes instead of human flesh that
    Winnie-the-Pooh and Little Women ate.
Innocent children have no use for fables about rabbits
    or donkeys or tortoises or porpoises,
What they want is something with plenty of
    well-mutilated corpoises.

Not on legends of how the rose came to be a rose
   instead of a petunia is their fancy fed,
But on the inside story of how somebody's bones got
   ground up to make somebody else's bread.
They'll go to sleep listening to the story of the little
   beggarmaid who got to be queen by being kind to
   the bees and the birds,
But they're all eyes and ears the minute they suspect a
   wolf or a giant is going to tear some poor
   woodcutter into quarters or thirds.
It doesn't take much to fill their cup;
All they want is for somebody to be eaten up.
Therefore I say unto you, all you poets who are so
   crazy about meek and mild little children and their
   angelic air,
If you are sincere and really want to please them,
   why not just go out and get yourselves

                              devoured by a bear.

The Cow

The cow is of the bovine ilk;
One end is moo, the other, milk.

The Pig

The pig, if I am not mistaken,
Supplies us with sausage, ham and bacon.
Let others say his heart is big –
I call it stupid of the pig.

The Egg

Let's think of eggs.
They have no legs.
Chickens come from eggs
But they have legs.
The plot thickens;
Eggs come from chickens,
But have no legs under 'em.
What a conundrum!

The Duck

Behold the duck.
It does not cluck.
A cluck it lacks.
It quacks.
It is specially fond
Of a puddle or a pond.
When it dines or sups,
It bottoms ups.

The Turkey

There is nothing more perky
Than a masculine turkey.
When he struts he struts
With no ifs or buts.
When his face is apoplectic
His harem grows hectic,
And when he gobbles
Their universe wobbles.

A Watched Example Never Boils

The weather is so very mild
That some would call it warm.
Good gracious, aren't we lucky, child?
Here comes a thunderstorm.

The sky is now indelible ink,
The branches reft asunder;
But you and I, we do not shrink;
We love the lovely thunder.

The garden is a raging sea,
The hurricane is snarling;
Oh happy you and happy me!
Isn't the lightning darling?

Fear not the thunder, little one.
It's weather, simply weather;
It's friendly giants full of fun
Clapping their hands together.

I hope of lightning our supply
Will never be exhausted;
You know it's lanterns in the sky
For angels who are losted.

We love the kindly wind and hail,
The jolly thunderbolt,
We watch in glee the fairy trail
Of ampere, watt, and volt.

Oh, than to enjoy a storm like this
There's nothing I would rather.
Don't dive beneath the blankets, Miss!
Or else leave room for Father.

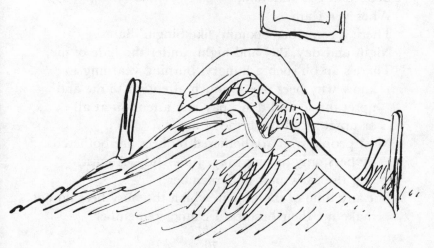

There is obviously a complete lack of understanding
    between the bee
And me.
You can't say Please
To bees.
At least, no matter with how many pleases your speech is
    bedecked,
It doesn't have any effect.
This is the simple truth that I unwilling found,
From bees following me around.
Bees cease their booming to and fro
To boom where I go;
Wherever I come,
Bees come too and hum;
Wherever I am,
There is some bee boomin' like Singin' Sam.
Night and day, day and night, under the hide of me,
There's an oh such a hungry, burning yearning to
    know why bees pay so much attention to me and
    upset me so and don't pay any attention at all
    or upset at all the bride of me,
Most people who are bothered by bees are bothered
    by bees only during May, June, July, August,
    and the early part of September,
But any time of the year in which the busy bees do not
    make me their business I cannot remember.

They are like the United States Mails, for the elements
   mean nothing to them,
And my garments are of what they wish to be in the
   vicinity of the hem,
And there is no sanctuary indoors,
For the room has not been built which I can enter
   without some bee which has been tuning up its motor,
   well, suddenly into life it roars,
And roses are red and violets are blue,
And that's what the bees ought to eat, but whatever
   I am eating they want to eat it too,
And I think that bees are what my idea of life is
   owing to,
Because no bee has stung me yet but I always think
   that every bee I meet, and I meet a lot of bees,
   is going to,
And so I am ridden through life with bees in the saddle
   and stirrup,
So you take the honey if you want, but I'll take
   maple syrup.

Sweet Dreams

I wonder as into bed I creep
What it feels like to fall asleep.
I've told myself stories, I've counted sheep,
But I'm always asleep when I fall asleep.
Tonight my eyes I will open keep,
And I'll stay awake till I fall asleep,
Then I'll know what it feels like to fall asleep,
Asleep,
Asleeep,
Asleeeep . . .

The Eel

I don't mind eels
Except as meals.
And the way they feels.

The Shrimp

A shrimp who sought his lady shrimp
Could catch no glimpse,
Not even a glimp.
At times, translucence
Is rather a nuisance.

The Jellyfish

Who wants my jellyfish?
I'm not sellyfish!

The Guppy

Whales have calves,
Cats have kittens,
Bears have cubs,
Bats have bittens;
Swans have cygnets,
Seals have puppies,
But guppies just have little guppies.

The Squid

What happy appellations these
Of birds and beasts in companies!
A shrewdness of apes, a sloth of bears,
A sculk of foxes, a huske of hares.
An exaltation 'tis of larks,
And possibly a grin of sharks,
But I declare a squirt of squid
I should not like to be amid.
Skin divers boldly swim through sepia,
But I can think of nothing creepier.

The Octopus

Tell me, O Octopus, I begs,
Is those things arms, or is they legs?
I marvel at thee, Octopus;
If I were thou, I'd call me Us.

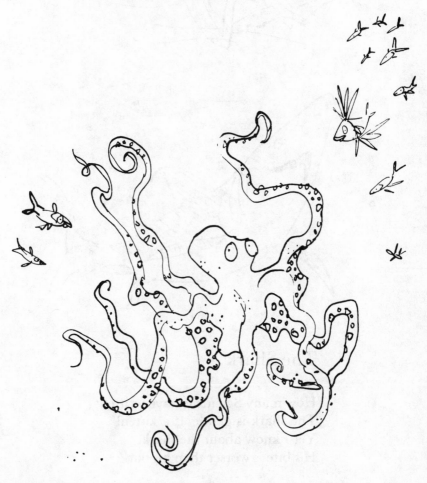

The Shark

How many Scientists have written
The shark is gentle as a kitten!
Yet I know about the shark:
His bite is worser than his bark.

The Porpoise

I kind of like the playful porpoise,
A healthy mind in a healthy corpus.
He and his cousin, the playful dolphin,
Why they like swimmin like I like golphin.

The Adventures of Isabel

Isabel met an enormous bear,
Isabel, Isabel, didn't care;
The bear was hungry, the bear was ravenous,
The bear's big mouth was cruel and cavernous.
The bear said, Isabel, glad to meet you,
How do, Isabel, now I'll eat you!
Isabel, Isabel, didn't worry,
Isabel didn't scream or scurry,
She washed her hands and she straightened her
    hair up,
Then Isabel quietly ate the bear up.

Once in a night as black as pitch
Isabel met a wicked witch.
The witch's face was cross and wrinkled,
The witch's gums with teeth were sprinkled.
Ho ho, Isabel! the old witch crowed,
I'll turn you into an ugly toad!
Isabel, Isabel, didn't worry,
Isabel didn't scream or scurry,
She showed no rage, she showed no rancor,
But she turned the witch into milk and drank her.

Isabel met a hideous giant,
Isabel continued self-reliant.
The giant was hairy, the giant was horrid,
He had one eye in the middle of his forehead.
Good morning, Isabel, the giant said,
I'll grind your bones to make my bread.
Isabel, Isabel, didn't worry,
Isabel didn't scream or scurry.
She nibbled the zwieback that she always fed off,
And when it was gone, she cut the giant's head off.

Isabel met a troublesome doctor,
He punched and he poked till he really shocked her.
The doctor's talk was of coughs and chills
And the doctor's satchel bulged with pills.
The doctor said unto Isabel,
Swallow this, it will make you well.
Isabel, Isabel, didn't worry,
Isabel didn't scream or scurry.
She took those pills from the pill concoctor,
And Isabel calmly cured the doctor.

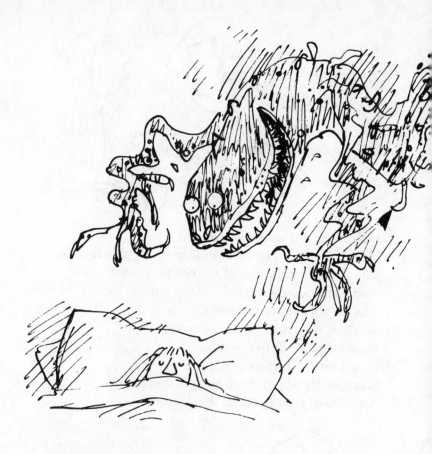

Isabel once was asleep in bed
When a horrible dream crawled into her head.
It was worse than a dinosaur, worse than a shark,
Worse than an octopus oozing in the dark.
'Boo!' said the dream, with a dreadful grin,
'I'm going to scare you out of your skin!'
Isabel, Isabel, didn't worry,
Isabel didn't scream or scurry,
Isabel had a cleverer scheme;
She just woke up and fooled that dream.

Whenever you meet a bugaboo
Remember what Isabel used to do.
Don't scream when the bugaboo says 'Boo!'
Just look it in the eye and say, 'Boo to you!'
That's how to banish a bugaboo;
Isabel did it and so can you!
Boooooo to you.

Next!

I thought that I would like to see
The early world that used to be,
That mastodonic mausoleum,
The Natural History Museum.
At midnight in the vasty hall
The fossils gathered for a ball.
High above notices and bulletins
Loomed up the Mesozoic skeletons.
Aroused by who knows what elixirs,
They ground along like concrete mixers.

They bowed and scraped in reptile pleasure,
And then began to tread the measure.
There were no drums or saxophones,
But just the clatter of their bones,
A rolling, rattling carefree circus
Of mammoth polkas and mazurkas.
Pterodactyls and brontosauruses
Sang ghostly prehistoric choruses.
Amid the megalosauric wassail
I caught the eye of one small fossil.
Cheer up, old man, he said, and winked –
It's kind of fun to be extinct.

Custard the Dragon and the Wicked Knight

Guess what happened in the little white house
Where Belinda lived with a little grey mouse,
And a kitten, and a puppy, and a little red wagon,
And a realio, trulio, little pet dragon.

This dragon was a shy one, for ever getting flustered,
So they said he was a coward, and they called him
   Custard.
He had eaten up a pirate once, but then
He went back to being a coward again.

Custard the dragon felt comfortable and cozy,
His breath wasn't fiery, just flickery and rosy,
And he lay with his head on his iron dragon toes,
Dreaming dragon dreams in a happy dragon doze.

Belinda sang as she went about her housework,
Blink the mouse was busy with her mousework,
Ink the kitten was laundering her fur,
And teaching the little dog Mustard to purr.

Belinda's song, as she wiped the dishes bright,
Was all about Sir Garagoyle, the wicked, wicked knight.
His castle's on a mountain, above the edelweiss;
Its gates are solid iron, its walls are solid ice;
And underneath the cellar is the dismalest of caves,
Where he keeps the captive maidens he has carried off
    as slaves.

Ink, Blink and Mustard joined their voices three:
'We're not cowardly like Custard, we're courageous
    as can be.
So hush you, Belinda, hush you, do not fret you.
We promise that Sir Garagoyle shall never, never
    get you.'
Then – just as Ink was complimenting Blink –
'That', said a voice, 'is what *you* think!'

Belinda dropped the dishes on the floor,
For there was Sir Garagoyle, coming in the door.
You could tell he was wicked, for he reeked of roguery,
He was like an ogre, only twice as ogre-y,
He was twice as big as a big gorilla,
And covered with armor like an armadilla –
Armor on the front of him, armor on the back,
And every inch of it thunderstorm-black.
Ink got gooseflesh, Blink was terror-laden,
And Mustard yelped that *he* was not a maiden.
Blink fled downstairs, Ink fled up,
And underneath the sofa went the pup.

Sir Garagoyle pounced with panther speed
And carried off Belinda on his snorting steed.
He plied his spurs with a cruel heel;
He was in a hurry for his evening meal,
His favorite meal, of screws and nails
And rattlesnake tongues and crocodile tails.

Custard was roused from his quiet dreams
By the pitiful sound of Belinda's screams.
'To horse!' he cried. 'Brave friends, to horse!
We must organise a Rescue Force!'
Said Mustard, 'I'd show that wicked knight -
But I've got a toothache and I couldn't bite.'

Said Ink, 'I can hardly stir my stumps;
I'm afraid that I'm coming down with mumps.'
Said Blink, 'If only I were feeling brisker . . .!
But I'm weakened by an ingrowing whisker.'

'Alas,' said Custard, 'alas, poor Belinda!'
He sighed a sigh, and the sigh was a cinder.
'Her three brave bodyguards are powerless as she,
And no one to rescue her but chickenhearted me.
Well,' said Custard, 'at least I'm in the mood
To be the toughest chicken that was ever chewed.'

As he thought about Belinda and Sir Garagoyle
Everything inside him began to boil.
He sizzled and he simmered and he bubbled and
   he hissed,
Then he whooshed like a rocket through the
   evening mist.

With headlight eyes and spikes a-bristle
He pierced the air like a locomotive whistle,
Then swooped from the sky as grim as fate
And knocked on Garagoyle's fearsome gate.

Sir Garagoyle rose at Custard's hail:
He was chewing a screw and swallowing a nail.
He called, 'You can hammer all night and day,
But you might as well take yourself away.
My gates are iron and my walls are ice,
And I've woven a spell around them thrice,
And if by chance you should break in,
I'll lay you open from tail to chin.'

He thought to frighten the dragon to death,
But Custard blew like a blowtorch breath.
He was a small volcano with the whooping cough,
And like molten lava the gates flowed off!
He blew another breath, and the icy walls
Came a-splashing down in waterfalls.

Sir Garagoyle spluttered like a sprinkler-wagon,
'A knight can always beat a dragon!'
'Pooh!' said Custard. 'How you rant!
A true knight could, but a wicked knight can't.'
'Have at you then!' Sir Garagoyle roared,
And he rushed at Custard with his deadly sword.

Twice Custard parried those fierce attacks,
Then he swung his tail like a battle axe.
From helm and breastplate down to spur
It flattened that unworthy Sir.
His armor crumpled like thin tinfoil,
And that was the end of Garagoyle.

Custard rushed like a tidal wave
Down, down, down to the dismal cave
Where Belinda lay in chains, a slave –
Chains too strong to chop or hack,
But he sawed them through with his spiky back.
Belinda was too weak to speak her thanks,
But she managed to pat his scaly flanks.

Now, Custard was a flyer of great renown,
He was able to fly while sitting down,
So home he soared with wings a-flap,
And Belinda sitting in his lap.
Ink, Blink and Mustard were in a happy tizzy,
They danced around Belinda till they made her dizzy,
Then they looked at Custard and they gave a shout:
'There's a rabbit in the kitchen, and he won't get out.
He's eaten all the carrots and he's starting on the peas,
And you're just in time to eject him, please!'

Custard said, 'You know my habits;
You know I've *always* been afraid of rabbits;
So if this fierce fellow won't depart in peace,
Eject him yourself or call the police.'
'Oh,' jeered Ink and Blink and Mustard,
'What a cowardly, cowardly, cowardly Custard!'
'I agree,' said Custard; 'and I add to that
Craven, poltroon, and fraidy-cat.
I've learned what a nuisance bravery can be,
So a coward's life is the life for me.'
Belinda kissed him and said, 'Don't fret,
A cowardly dragon makes the nicest pet.'

The Cherub

I like to watch the clouds roll by,
And think of cherubs in the sky;
But when I think of cherubim,
I don't know if they're her or him.

The People Upstairs

The people upstairs all practice ballet.
Their living room is a bowling alley.
Their bedroom is full of conducted tours.
Their radio is louder than yours.
They celebrate week-ends all the week.
When they take a shower, your ceilings leak.
They try to get their parties to mix
By supplying their guests with Pogo sticks,
And when their orgy at last abates,
They go to the bathroom on roller skates.
I might love the people upstairs wondrous
If instead of above us, they just lived under us.

German Song

The German children march along,
Heads full of fairy tales and song.
They read of witches in their reader,
They sing of angels in their lieder.
I think their little heads must swim;
The songs are jolly, the tales are Grimm.

Russian Dance

The Russian moujik is made for music,
For music the moujik is most enthusic.
Whenever an instrument twangs or toots
He tucks his trousers into his boots,
He squats on his heels, but his knees don't crack,
And he kicks like a frenzied jumping jack.
My knees would make this performance tragic,
But his have special moujik magic.

The Polka

Hop step step step,
Hop step step step,
Go the Polish dancers.
Polka or mazurka?
I wish I knew the answers.
Such names to me sound rigmarolish,
I must polish up my Polish.

Arabian Dance

The sultan lies when day is spent
On silken cushions in silken tent.
Before him silken dancers twine,
Sinuous and serpentine,
And silken courtiers, silent never,
Chant, 'O Sultan, live for ever!'
The vizier lurks behind his lord,
Fingering a silken cord.

The Big Tent Under the Roof

Noises new to sea and land
Issue from the circus band.
Each musician looks like mumps
From blowing umpah umpah umps.

Lovely girls in spangled pants
Ride on gilded elephants.
Elephants are useful friends,
They have handles on both ends;

They hold each other's hindmost handles
And flee from mice and Roman candles;
Their hearts are gold, their hides are emery,
And they have a most tenacious memory.

Notice also, girls and boys,
The circus horses' avoirdupois.
Far and wide the wily scouts
Seek these snow-white stylish stouts.
Calmer steeds were never found
Unattached to a merry-go-round.
Equestriennes prefer to jump
Onto horses pillow-plump.

Equestriennes will never ride
As other people do, astride.
They like to balance on one foot,
And wherever they get, they won't stay put.
They utter frequent whoops and yips,
And have the most amazing hips.
Pink seems to be their favorite color,
And very few things are very much duller.

Yet I for one am more than willing
That everything should be less thrilling.
My heart and lungs both bound and balk
When high-wire walkers start to walk.
They ought to perish, yet they don't;
Some fear they will, some fear they won't.

I lack the adjectives, verbs and nouns
To do full justice to the clowns.
Their hearts are constantly breaking, I hear,
And who am I to interfere?
I'd rather shake hands with **Mr Ringling**
And tell him his circus is a beautiful thingling.

The Purist

I give you now Professor Twist,
A conscientious scientist,
Trustees exclaimed, 'He never bungles!'
And sent him off to distant jungles.
Camped on a tropic riverside,
One day he missed his loving bride.
She had, the guide informed him later,
Been eaten by an alligator.
Professor Twist could not but smile.
'You mean,' he said, 'a crocodile.'

The Lion

Oh, weep for Mr and Mrs Bryan!
He was eaten by a lion;
Following which, the lion's lioness
Up and swallowed Bryan's Bryaness.

A Caution to Everybody

Consider the auk;
Becoming extinct because he forgot how to fly,
  and could only walk.
Consider man, who may well become extinct
Because he forgot how to walk and learned
  how to fly before he thinked.

The Wombat

The wombat lives across the seas,
Among the fair Antipodes.
He may exist on nuts and berries,
Or then again, on missionaries;
His distant habit precludes
Conclusive knowledge of his moods.
But I would not engage the wombat
In any form of mortal combat.

The Grynch

I dearly love the three-toed grynch,
It grows upon me inch by inch.
Each home with one should be provided;
The Lord did not create it, so I did.
It's useful for closing conversations
With stubborn salesmen and poor relations.
Long-winded storytellers flinch
If I bring up the three-toed grynch.
When I speak of the grynch which I adore
I'm a bore, I'm a bore, I'm a fabulous bore.
But so can life be; in a pinch,
I recommend the three-toed grynch.

Everybody has an Uncle

I wish I were a Tibetan monk
Living in a monastery.
I would unpack my trunk
And store it in a tronastery;
I would collect all my junk
And send it to a jonastery;
I would try to reform my unc-
le and pay his expenses at an onastery,
And if my income shrunk
I would send it to a shronastery.

The Skink

Let us do justice to the skink
Who isn't what so many think.
On consultation with a wizard
I find the skink a kind of lizard.
Since he is not a printer's whim,
Don't sniff and back away from him,
Or you may be adjudged too drunk
To tell a lizard from a skunk.

The Bat

Myself, I rather like the bat,
It's not a mouse, it's not a rat.
It has no feathers, yet has wings,
It's quite inaudible when it sings.
It zigzags through the evening air
And never lands on ladies' hair,
A fact of which men spend their lives
Attempting to convince their wives.

The Praying Mantis

From whence arrived the praying mantis?
From outer space, or lost Atlantis?
I glimpse the grim, green metal mug
That masks this pseudo-saintly bug,
Orthopterous, also carnivorous,
And faintly whisper, Lord deliver us.

The Centipede

I objurgate the centipede,
A bug we do not really need.
At sleepy-time he beats a path
Straight to the bedroom or the bath.
You always wallop where he's not,
Or, if he is, he makes a spot.

The Ant

The ant has made himself illustrious
Through constant industry industrious.
So what?
Would you be calm and placid
If you were full of formic acid?

The Carcajou and the Kincajou

They tell me of a distant zoo
Where a carcajou met a kincajou.
Full soon to savage blows they came
From laughing at each other's name.
The agile ajous fought till dark
And carc slew kinc and kinc slew carc,
And beside the conquered kincajou
Lay the carcass of the carcajou.

The Wapiti

There goes the Wapiti,
Hippety-hoppity!

Sources

The poems included in this collection were originally published as follows:

'The Cow' (1931) 'The Cobra' (1931) 'To a Small Boy Standing on My Shoes While I am Wearing Them' (1931) in *Free Wheeling* (1931); 'The Pig' (1933) 'The Parent' (1933) 'The Rhinoceros' (1932) 'The Cat' (1933) 'The Wapiti' (1933) in *Happy Days* (1933); 'It's Never Fair Weather' (1933) 'The Germ' (1933) 'Don't Cry Darling, It's Blood All Right' (1934) 'The Clean Platter' (1935) 'There's Obviously a Complete Lack of Understanding . . .' (1935) 'The Wombat' (1933) 'There was a young lady named Harris' (1935) 'There was an old man in a trunk' (1935) 'Fame was a claim of Uncle Ed's' (1935) in *The Primrose Path* (1935); 'The Tale of Custard the Dragon' (1936) 'Epistle to the Olympians' (1936) 'The Camel' (1933) 'The Adventures of Isabel' (1936) 'The Big Tent Under the Roof' (1936) 'A Watched Example Never Boils' (1936) in *The Bad Parents' Garden of Verse* (1936); 'I'll Get One Tomorrow' (1935) 'The Hippopotamus' (1935) 'The Purist' (1935) 'The Ant' (1935) in *I'm a Stranger Here Myself* (1935); 'The Turtle' (1940) in *Verses From 1929 On* (1930, 1945, 1959); 'The Kitten' (1940) 'The Canary' (1940) 'The Panther' (1940) 'The Centipede' (1935) in *The Face is Familiar* (1940); 'The Sniffle' (1941) 'The Termite' (1942) 'The Kangaroo' (1942) 'You and Me and P. B. Shelley' (1942) 'The Octopus' (1942) 'The Shark' (1942) 'The Porpoise' (1942) 'The Jellyfish' (1942) 'The Eel' (1942) 'The Parsnip' (1941) 'Celery' (1941) 'The Skink' (1942) 'The Panda' (1942) in *Good Intentions* (1942); 'The Duck' (1936) 'The Turkey' (1935) in *Many Long Years Ago* (1945); 'Tableau at Twilight' (1942) 'The Lion' (1944) 'The Cherub' (1944) 'The Guppy' (1944) 'The People Upstairs' (1949) 'The Porcupine' (1944) in *Verus* (1949); 'Everybody has an Uncle' (1938) in *Family Reunion* (1950); 'The Wendigo' (1952) 'A Caution to Everybody' (1950) 'The Grynch' (1952) 'I often grieve for Uncle Hannibal' (1950) 'Next!' (1952) 'The Mules' (1952) 'The Bat' (1952) 'The Toucan' (1952) in *Private Dining Room* (1952); 'Can I Get You a Glass of Water' or 'Please Close the Glottis After You' (1953) 'The Ostrich' (1956) 'The Squid' (1956) 'The Egg' (1936) 'The Pizza' (1957) 'The Praying Mantis' (1956) in *You Can't Get There From Here* (1957); 'Between Birthdays' (1961) 'Russian Dance' (1961) 'Arabian Dance' (1961) 'The Polka' (1961) 'German Song' (1961) 'Winter Morning' (1961) 'Sweet Dreams' (1961) in *New Nutcracker Suite and Other Innocent Verses* (1962); 'Custard the Dragon and the Wicked Knight' (1961) in *Custard the Dragon and the Wicked Knight* (1962); 'Jack Do-Good-for-Nothing' (1962) 'The Dog' (1962) 'The Shrimp' (1962) 'The Beefburger' (1957) 'Mustard' (1957) 'The Carcajou and the Kincajou' (1962) in *Everyone But Me and Thee* (1962).